Torn from the Ear of Night

Torn from the Ear of Night

Jimmie Margaret Gilliam

Edited by Paula Paradise

WHITE PINE PRESS / BUFFALO, NEW YORK

White Pine Press
P.O. Box 236
Buffalo, New York 14201

www.whitepine.org

Acknowledgments: Some of these poems first appeared in *Buffalo Journal, Black Mountain Review I, Black Mountain Review II, Earth's Daughters,* and *The Buffalo News.* Many of them appeared in the books *The Rime & Roar of Revolution* (Friends of Malatesta, Buffalo, New York) *Ain't No Bears Out Tonight* (White Pine Press, Buffalo, New York), and *Pieces of Bread* (White Pine Press, Dreamseasons and Serendipity Arts, Buffalo, New York)

Publication of this book was made possible, in part, by public funds from the New York State Council on the Arts with the support of Governor Andrew M. Cuomo and the New York State Legislature, a State Agency, and by the generosity of the donors listed in the back of this volume.

Cover art: *Moonlight on the Mountain* by Mary Taglieri. Used by permission of the artist.

Printed and bound in the United States of America.

ISBN 978-1-935210-92-4

Library of Congress number 2016957098

CONTENTS

ADOLESCENCE

LOVE

ACROSS TIME AND SPACE

for you

Pardon me, if when I want
To tell the story of my life
It's the land I talk about.
This is the land.
It grows in your blood
And you grow.
If it dies in your blood
You die out.

—Pablo Neruda,
    from *Still Another Day*,
    translated by William O'Daly

Time stands still
in the eye of writing storm
no wonder we struggle
so hard to get there
if it were easy
we might never come back

Love Made Me

Debora Ott

Jimmie Margaret Gilliam loved to drive. Pedal to metal, her writing process held fast to life's curves, its tread and promise. And so at the end, the making of this book engaged her in onward days. Notes scrawled on sections of the *New York Times* stashed under the sunroom table, saved copies of *The New Yorker*. Her research stacked towering toward tomorrow.

She was born between the Blue Ridge and Smoky Mountains in "The Land of the Sky" eight miles from the town of Asheville, North Carolina. *What was constant in our lives was Nature herself—her changing seasons in a place of breath-taking beauty.* She cared deeply about the Earth—and what gets created there. Yet she was clear she was not a Southern writer.

Jimmie came to writing from being born into an oral culture where telling stories was akin to breathing, and she came to writing from loving to read. She began writing with intent in her mid-thirties, and started to think of herself as a serious poet in the 1980s when I invited her to read with poets Lorna Dee Cervantes and Marge Piercy for Just Buffalo literary center. She was most happy when moving through chaos—the raw materials of life, mind, emotions into harmony, completeness, serenity; and the making of a poem for her was one important way of experiencing that movement.

Jimmie considered the Self a valid land for her poetic vision, even as her eyes looked outward. *A good poem, for me, is a golden map of one's interior life from which the outer world can be recreated... It dares chart new dreams infused with organic life that moves toward authentic survival ——not just making do/getting by.* Her vision swept upward from subconscious psychic roots, that long way; and her poems came with that movement. *I see the blood of my childhood through/into the bone of my womanhood.*

Graveside

I go to your grave, Mother
The car makes the hillside curve
At Pisgah View
Stops at the magnolia tree
I am alone
Your bones nudge the scab of my hidden tears
I weep within the rain
I walk to your place   sideways
As I once approached the Pacific Ocean
At Cape Disappointment, Oregon

I am your daughter on the way to the store
To buy cornmeal   to fry okra
From Rhobena's garden

I have much to say to you, Mother
But now there is only time to arrange the silk flowers
Limp in the rain
I entwine two of them
One red, one pale purple
I do not tell you
Daddy has mowed down your lilacs
The rosebud bush

Your death still takes my legs away, Mother
But I walk on the air/my will
Away from the mirror you hold for me
Deep in the earth

I am your poet, Mother
Though my words do not grace your ears
I am bone of your bone
You stand in my frame
Bone catches in the throat
Of this grief

—from *Pieces of Bread*

As a poet, Jimmie found language that began with the senses—*flesh made word, a connecting of body and mind. . . to bridge the landscape of the unconscious to the conscious ground. . .* and believed the *poem lifts, causes to surface, an incredible personal energy which in turn generates all kinds of making within the world. Huge chunks of insight, imagery, emotion, rhythms are unearthed, which fuel our acts. The poem becomes a repository for psychic power which can release imagination.* She wanted her poems to generate an arc of connection with the reader. She was a pacifist, a pluralist, a patient and inspiring teacher whose sense of community and spirit of generosity ran wide and wild and deep.

. . .until whole communities
will choose beauty over destruction
life over death. . .
the choice is based
on desire

Beneath her cool and calm lay ferocity and a valiant soul's drive for connection. Peddling icy Buffalo streets one Valentine's Day, she delivered longstem roses from her bicycle basket. The blood red blooms darkened by the cold nevertheless passed warm and open-handed into the palms of those she loved.

Jimmie was a single mom like me, and her beloved Jill and Jenny were about a dozen or more years older than my Alice and Sabina. She was Auntie to them, and I sought her advice more than once during times of revolt and revolution. *Let her live*, she said, unknowingly echoing the immigrant women's shouts to my grandmother during their Atlantic crossing when my mother, then seven, let slip her mother's coral necklace into the roiling sea.

Jimmie allowed for missteps and knew, as the immigrant women did, that the values we place and nurture in our children remain and return. Her openness to the diverse possibilities of what it meant to be woman and fully human, to be alive in a world not yet ready for one's passion and power, gave rise to work she wrested from silence.

Many years ago, I invited Jimmie to teach a workshop called The Translation of Silence, because she believed that *so many of the lives of women are buried by silence, a silence carefully hidden by layers of fear, anger and shame, often within a self-imposed repression.* She knew that *beneath all those thick walls lies a passionate voice wanting to convert to life. If my poems can evoke the desire to open that expression, I will have fulfilled my own hope for my work in the world.*

I have a photo Jimmie gave me years ago. She's standing next to a painted wood sign at City Lights Bookstore in San Francisco that reads, "I AM THE DOOR." And I think of her that way, as a portal, opening the way in or out to parts of ourselves, enabling us to recognize our life's work and get it done.

I care about you; we must write the blood of our childhood through. . .I offer my poems for marking, if not finding, that way.

Clear and at ease, no compulsion to please, this Appalachian-born woman broke silence, her breath waking hollers like mountain wind, for you.

Author's note: All the words that appear in italics are Jimmie Margaret's.

Ancestry

"well that sure harelips the governor"
—Lucy's old expression

From left to right front row:
Little Lucy (in Emma's lap), Johnson, Joe Halford (your father, his back
turned, Annie straightforward at the end
Emma (mother, sitting) Minnie (standing) outlives all of you
And finally one-eyed Leah, right "business eye" intact

Jimmie's Notes:

Emma dead before forty— Why?
Johnson run over by a train in his twenties
Paw Paw Halford lives on into his eighties (what influence?)
Annie (Norma Ray) "foreman" in the South Carolina Mills (Pacolet, S.C.)
Dies of a heart attack
Went out on her broken porch
Leg went through broken boards
Minnie survives daughter's suicide
Lives into her eighties—will not die
Outlives everyone (made up her mind)
Leah died in the asylum at thirty-nine

The Worn Photo

Little Lucy sits on her mother's lap. Emma's long hand keeps her within the circle of her right arm and hand. The child's arms are crossed. Her oval eyes turn up at the edges; they are shaped like teardrops. The small girl's gaze is reflective—outside the space framed in the picture—as if she knows within weeks her mother will be dead.

She wears a crocheted jacket. Bows pull back her hair parted in middle. The sepia tones in the worn photograph mute the rich brown-reds of her chestnut hair, but it is these eyes and those full cheeks which do not dimple that say *I am an old child*, her face registering her mother's tired hold on life.

Seven babies later, two who die in her womb, Emma poses with her family for her last picture. She will die in the night holding little Lucy in her arms. The child hears the death rattle, cries for Mama the next morning when she wakes alone.

After Emma dies, Joe Halford takes the picture to Spartanburg. "My Emma is gone," he tells the photographer. "Please take her likeness from this picture you took in the spring; make me a portrait of my wife—make it as large as life." Joe hangs the picture over his bed. At night he retires to memory's warm body. In the morning he comforts the sobbing child.

A Time Before Sorrow

I always wondered where we came from—me and Joann and Mother and Daddy. "Are we Irish?" I'd ask when I grew up. "Are we English?"

No one would ever answer me. When my first grown-up friend, the Reverend E.W. Black, our Wesleyan pastor, died, I heard the words, "Ashes to ashes, dust to dust" at his grave and I decided we had come out of the dirt.

My daddy and my mother must have come full grown from the flowing broomsage next to the little house. Their importance to me would not allow them to have ever been small. My first memory of myself was standing in front of Mother's three-mirror dresser in her bedroom. Though I did not yet know how to walk, I would stand for hours at the shelf at the bottom of the long middle mirror holding onto the shelf that connected the three drawers on either side of my mother's dresser; above each set of drawers were mirrors which folded inward like wings. I would pull myself up from crawling to look at the child in the mirror. Not yet a year old, I would say my handful of words at myself, turn my back to me, and take my first steps. I followed this ritual until my legs no longer needed me to talk myself into letting go. I figured I was born nine months old, that mother's mirror dresser was my womb.

My big baby doll, almost as big as I—the one Aunt Vi gave me when Paw Paw Gilliam died—was the only "baby" I'd been around so when Joann was born when I was four I heard someone say she came out of an egg. Since she weighed over eight pounds I pictured something like Humpty Dumpty. That was before Aunt Evelyn dropped her and she didn't break.

When I was a child I felt like my magic slate with its liftable sheet of cellophane; everyone left their words on me. But a day outside at the trunk of the old, oak tree playing with June bugs and acorns, ants and butterflies, lightning bugs and crickets, swept my mind clear.

The Bible verse I memorized at Sunday school from the book of Genesis said, "In the beginning was the word," but I knew at the heart of my childhood lay a time before sorrow, in a land without words.

I could show you this place in a Kodak box camera snapshot, crinkled from squeezing it in my hand when I was a two-year-old and carried it around with me all day and slept with it at night. In the picture my mother and daddy are standing on a rock wall. Their faces are turned to each other, their heads high above an invisible horizon against a white sky. When I grew up I would learn the picture was taken a mile high up at Clingman's Dome in the Smokies. In the picture, they are kissing each other on the mouth. "That's when I was born," thought the three-year-old. I am a daughter of "the land of the sky."

The place where I was born in the Carolina hills smelled of hemlock, white pine, and cedar. The spring pink and white of the dogwood and its red berries in the fall taught me seasons. What a girl was came clear in the throat of a purple/blue iris. Before I was afraid of the woods, the twin tulip poplar was my favorite. I learned passion from mountain lightning's forked tongues. Thunder and woodpeckers taught me rhythm. Sunset and dawn were brother and sister, like tone and like nuance. Cardinals, bluebirds, and crows taught me song, while mockingbirds mimicked me.

The earth was my poem, my body, my home, woven of clay, flint, breath, voice, and word.

Torn From the Ear of Night

The child opens her eyes
Like any other morning:
From the trundle bed her daddy made
With its matching nightstand
Same height as her three-year-old self
She hears her sister's footfalls
Her daddy's moving around

She doesn't remember last night
Falling asleep in her mother's lap
In the big oak rocker
With the regularity of its squeak,
Squeak, squeak, squeak…

She calls out,
Mama, Mama, Mama

Her daddy stoops through the doorway
Sits in the chair beside her bed
Leans to her:
Oh Lucy, our little lady,
Mama's gone, Mama's gone

The bruise on her childhood's heart
Turns purple in the dawning hour

Ever after between sleep and awakening
There lies a crinkly, grey path
The one she's not supposed to take—her fear a fluid sound
A sheet of tin makes
Rippling before it becomes
A roof over home

Dearest Emma

October, 1910
Bethlehem Community
Old Fort, North Carolina

Dearest Emma, Beloved Wife,

I used the mahogany I was saving to make us a dining room table for your coffin. Although my hands felt like wood, I fashioned beauty into your final bed.

The lamp's light fell in circles on the finished boards reminding me of the depth of your dark eyes. Your eyes were the first part of you to take me in.

Tomorrow we leave at first light for the trip back up into the mountains where you and I were born and raised. Missing the mountains and now missing you is too much for me to bear—I talked it over with the children as you would have wanted me to and they are on board to help me.

I held you, Emma, the night your breath caught—and never let itself out. The rest of the night I held you until my arms fell asleep. I helped your body lie down and then I put mine over yours—to lengthen what I hoped would be for you the feeling of being alive as long as your senses could grasp me.

I could not bear to close your eyes.

Leah says Mama's not dead, she's looking at me. We've fixed a pallet for you at the front of our buckboard wagon with a makeshift umbrella to shield your face. The children want to take turns sitting beside you. Leah holds your hand. Lucy and Johnson are near me so they don't fall out. We will reach my Daddy's home place with any luck before dark.

I put the first letter I ever penned to you beneath you undergarments near your heart. In it, you know, was a promise for life—now for eternity.

I bathed you, Darling, slowly…the way we bathed and splashed each other after lovemaking. I talked us through that solitary bathing—ever pushing your life to last a few hours longer—for me.

When the tears will come, I don't know. Lucy cries the scalding tears of a three-year-old calling Mama. Johnson snubs in the night in rhythms his soft crying won't release him from. Annie, our oldest, has slipped into your rhythms of taking care of us as easy as if you had offered her your wine-colored bathrobe. Minnie, our tiny bolt of energy, begs me to take her fishing. But Leah, Leah has scratched her face out of the family picture.

Your Beloved Husband,
Joe

the land was lost
no, sold, you say
nevertheless
gone
the land is gone

Leah

did you claw out the left side
of your face before or after Emma died?

the Halfords kill themselves
Rebecca said matter of fact
soon after we met (in the 1980s)

blonde, blue-eyed Leah
Rebecca says you would have
been ok today—just needed
vitamins

Beloved Daughter

Beloved Daughter,

This is the hardest news I've had to bear since Johnson was run over on the railroad tracks.

Your sister, Leah, has died. I'm on my way to Morganton to get her at the asylum. I'm not good with telephones, don't own one myself. Minnie and her husband, Bruce, offered me the use of theirs but I thought it kinder to have you imagine the sound of my voice rather than hear it at what might be an interruption in your new, married life.

When I last spent the day with Leah, we walked on the grounds—not arm and arm as you and I might have—Leah always shied away from touch. She would say things like, "Hugs feel good at first but end up hurting when I'm by myself."

I don't think Leah ever got over Mama's dying. She said, "When Lucy visited me and I was down in the basement where they put the sick and the dying, Lucy told me, 'Mama's waiting for you in heaven, Leah.' Then she went home to be with her husband."

I know that Leah accused you of scratching out her face in the family picture taken a few months before your mother died, but I always thought she did it—to disappear—die somehow with Mama. Leah was never right after that and she got worse after you ran off and got married. Leah was still talking, weak as she was from the pneumony about me getting her a release so she could go back to the old homeplace up there at Crooked Creek. If she'd said it once, when you moved with your husband to Asheville, she said it a hundred times—*"I just want to go back to the old homeplace to get a drink of water. I just want to go back to the old homeplace to get a drink of water."*

When the sheriff stopped her that first time in the night, she was walking along the side of the road from Marion to Bethlehem and that's all she would say, *"I just want to get a drink of water at the old homeplace up the hill behind the springhouse."*

Every time I heard it something sunk in my chest—I guess it was any hope for peace I might have. That idea she'd fixed on, the regularity of her way of saying those words, her slipping off into the night—moonlight or no moonlight—I guess that's what finally compelled me to get her help.

Dearest Lucy, come, please, as soon as you can. Peace continues to elude your daddy. First I lost Emma to pneumony, then your brother, Johnson, to the night train—and now Leah—to a mind broken by thirst. Made worse by my decision. What harm would it have caused me to listen to her a thousand more times? *"I just want to go home to get a drink of water."*

With Love,
Your Daddy

Watermarks

Land. The word love struck me—a child of
near four. My mother screamed, cried without
stopping when the word came. Her niece, Virginia,
her sister's girl—beautiful dark-eyed, dark-haired,
dark Virginia—had driven into Lake James with
her lover. A double suicide. Her diary told the
simple classic: "If we can't live together, we will
die together." In love. Lake, was it a double
funeral?

He was a divorcee, her love. His love, she
was eighteen. Her father refused her seeing him.
She saw him; they talked over their lives,
strained-estranged. They made love in the car—
her father's *No* knotted in their minds, tightening
the intimacy unvoiced in their young throats.

The night they entered the water-moccasined waters
of Lake James, Bruce Parker had locked his daughter
out. Minnie, the small, frail, subtle mother, wept
cold tears in the bedroom away from the potbellied fire.

Love is danger—I was not taken to the funeral.
Ashes to dust. The chosen bed—Love dance within
Earth. Land.

Traveling Mercies

They baptized him James Noland
after his father/his mama
wouldn't let them
cut his hair/long black curls
He's too pretty to be a boy!

I was helpin' my daddy plow
by the time I was ten
Me and my daddy
took our horse, Ben
climbed all day across Old Fort Mountain
buckboard wagon hauling apples to sell in Asheville
through Black Mountain/camped by starlight
in the valley at Swannanoa

Noland drives his baby-blue Model-T Ford coupe
around hairpin curves
dirt road winding over Old Fort Mountain
(He was eighteen then)
drove the thirty-mile trip to study bookkeeping
married Lucy Margaret middle of the Roarin' Twenties
December 18, 1926 (they elope)
secretly set up housekeeping
turn their backs to Hickory Nut Gap
start a new road west.
Fifty-six years together/face Mt. Pisgah, the Smokies

Daddy and I sit near his fireplace
fire we've made/helping each other
record cold snap
We keep the fire goin' twenty-one nights/days

I've grown up/disappointed him
daughter who did not come back to live in the mountains
God's Country
to build a house next door to him
but we talk silence, weather,
time/if and when

Daddy, I came home Interstate 40
this time/up Old Fort Mountain
three-lane highway
took twenty minutes to Ridgecrest
came into Asheville via the new cut
bypassed Beaucatcher tunnel
where you and mother used to kiss
in front of us/tell us to make a wish
hold our breaths

Daddy brags/breaking his life's studied quiet:
I've seen four roads in my lifetime
across that mountain!
December 7, 1987
Daddy died today
leaving a rainbow on the land

Four roads across the mountain—
No: *five*

Noland

for my father

I hang my mind on the horse harness rack
in the barn.

I furrow feverishly you, sweet earth—

Then I sit unmoving in the motion of fields
Silent as a plow.

My Father Says Farewell to His Wife

I do not go with Daddy
back to Mother's room
at St. Joseph's Hospital
where moments earlier
she has died

You go with him
honor his slow effort to walk alone
dragging his right foot
long ago slowed
by the clot
in his left brain

Later you tell me
he bends to her body
kisses her
first on her forehead
then on her mouth
he presses his lips
into the hollow of her neck
loses his head in her bosom
then he howls

wild with amputation

My Father Sits in the Dark

My father sits
without any lights on
he says the lights are
eating him up

My daddy sits
deep in the dark
his wife is dead
he is conserving electricity

He has made what was
their home for fifty-six years

their shared tomb

We ask him
Are you getting eccentric
sitting here
night after night
alone with the lights out
he examines
the question carefully
straightens his slender back

No, I'm praying

Grace When Bone Gives Way

My father rides
a humble horse
His crooked foot
plows the stubborn grave

His withered hand
holds up his wan greeting
his firm farewell

Stories Stacked on the Land

for Merrill Bowen

In "The Land of the Sky"
The long light
Afternoon sun shadows
Takes the Valley—
Rich bottom lands

A green riverbed
Moves slow as virginity
In the land of the land
The foothills east of
The Blue Ridge
Mountains older
Than the Himalayas

Old Fort, Cherry Springs
Crooked Creek, Mt. Hebron,
Bethlehem
A map of the Holy Land
Drawn in the Bible Belt
Placenames blood-deep
As well water
The passion of ancestors

My great-grandparents
On Daddy's side
John and Mary Fortune
Set up housekeeping
Beneath Mt. Mitchell's
Tallest peak

Love that stays together
That rare plant
John and Mary will not know
Split apart after forty years

John leaves the mountains
(Some may say Mary ran him off)
She the meanest woman
in McDowell County
He fathers six more children
Farther South
In Atlanta

But in his eighties
John comes back to North Ca'lina
Drinking a quart
Straight whiskey a day
Determines to see
His Mary, his mountain
One more time

Eagle eye to eagle eye
They face each other

I hate you old woman
With a love that's kicked me
Blue all my life
But you'll spend eternity
With me Mary Coxey or else. . .

John Fortune, I'd go to hell first

graves face east
bodies positioned for
Jesus' coming

Graveside Sequel

we are not there, Mother
when they lower your coffin
through the thick gate
freezing rain
on top of the snowstorm
keeps us at the foot of the mountain

broken earth/your grave lies
quilted with flowers
enclosed in ice
lilies of the valley
Cordie's yellow rose
for faithfulness
gladiolas, mums
our roses, your beloved
violets

mountain iris/purple batons
you hand to me
I pass on to Jill and Jenny

You have made me
A grey coat/woven with sad threads
you would have me believe
guilt is the legacy of daughters
I dream you sit up at your funeral
accuse me/*you went off and left me*
               and I wasn't even dead

I lift your body through the red clay
sunlight breaks the iris
from their silver ice

I dress you in the Vogue dress
you drape a scarlet scarf
around your neck/sensuous
red flows
between your breasts/your legs

I can never compare with you, mother

It's time to give up the grave.

Childhood

Four Years Old at the A&P

for Masani Alexis De Veaux

My mother shops at the A&P
for the things we can't raise
on our small farm—
bananas, Fig Newtons,
white bread, mayonnaise

I slip away when she isn't looking
fill my pinafore pocket with bright berries

Turned loose by my mother's
frugal concentration
(She must account to my father for every penny)
I go up an aisle alone
the innocent thief

Skipping toward me
is a girl my size
eyes black as her shining face
her hair and her dress   *jazzy*   and red-ribboned
She's the cutest child I've ever seen
I want her to come home with me/be my sister
Eyes cling to eyes
I offer her my stolen fruit

When I hug her
all activity in the store stops
North of here
The Mason-Dixon line snaps like a whip
Water streams in opposite directions
at the Continental Divide
My mother pulls me back from my delight

To this day I rue the loss
within that round moment
at the A&P when we were
no less and no more than
two little girls
holding hands full of cranberries
not yet bruised by color

A Girl Blue as a Bluefish

Dr. Hensley delivers the baby
A girl blue as a bluefish
The umbilical cord wrapped around her neck
How can I tell them their child is...
Nurse Baumgartner's quick movement stops
His pronouncement
She repeats all the procedures
Clears the passages, nose and throat
Whacks the buttocks
Breathes into the stubborn lungs

I am that baby
She was my first friend
Her name is Glee

Posing at Cherokee with the Chief

Blank-faced and ignorant
As two acorns in knobby hats
We were taken as children
To the lands of the great Cherokee Nation

Through Maggie Valley
Up Soco Gap
Around and around hairpin curves
Past "the most photographed view"
In the Great Smokies

If we were lucky a she bear and her cubs
Will stop traffic at the overlook
We descend corkscrew curves
Ears popping cross the North Carolina state line
Into the Cherokee Reservation

FEED THE LIVE BEAR

BUY KODAK FILM

AUTHENTIC BEADS

MOCCASINS

Signs line the main street

HAVE YOUR PHOTO MADE WITH A REAL CHEROKEE CHIEF

The black and white snapshot
Cannot display his headdress
The brilliant feathers
But the picture captures the image
My awed hand in his

I bravely test his will—*to take or let me keep*
My curly scalp

Absorbed by his red-clay body
My five-year-old trembling self
Could not know his sweaty square hand
Was too young to belong
To the Chief of the Cherokee

I Could Lay Bare My Heart

for Jody

I.

I could lay bare
My heart to you, little sister
As long as I didn't cross
The line you draw
Down the middle
Of our mutual bed

When I make a teepee
With the broom handle under
Our covers in the night,
Flashlight in my chubby hand
Alice in Wonderland
In the other

II.

You, the sensitive one, me
The cowboy who made you be
The brave Indian—play dead
At the point of my drawn arrow

III.

It was clear to me early on—
Though I prayed every night
On my small knees for a brother
You were my playmate from heaven

I look out for you little sister
Like no other—
Take you to school, scare you with my stories
Teach you everything I know

Protect your gift
Your heart's pure gold

The Wounded Girl

Beneath my Shirley Temple curls
And blue taffeta hair bow
My head is sore and swollen
(from knocking it against the wall)
a penance I gladly pay
try to enter your dull stare
the lost brown of your eyes, Mother

> *you don't love me*
> *you don't understand me*
> *your daddy doesn't love me*
> *he doesn't understand me*
> *you don't love me*

I want to understand my mother
Her whirling mind/her head divided
But I die every time she looks up from the sewing machine
Fastens those words on me

I am at the mercy of her hands
My head jerked and banged with the hairbrush
Dog bite it! she explodes
Can't you even hold your head right?

Another time the same hands pat the top of my hair
Send champagne bubbles down my back

A deepening sorrow fills my mind
A sad well spills over
"Someone's got to be responsible"
I carve the unspeakable words
On the child's cave wall
"My mother's broken and I can't fix her"

Church Basement

i slowly
wee/wee/d around my pleasure
and slipping off
the cold commode seat
returned to the cement floor
to be in touch
with your wee wee against mine
tiny gun shooting chess
for the first time pawns

wide-eyed wide-legged
around our ecstasy
coming

until one of our mothers
called from the far side door
"what are you children doing?"

hiding inside the fists of ourselves
we clenched around each other
and trembling cried

we're playing church

but in the madness
of that scramble
to get the hell out into their light
the silver chalice
we were making
broke forever

and goes on breaking
                    breaking
                            breaking

Untitled

Me and Joann, little sisters
Lie to mother about throwing
Rocks at Glen David and Dixie
Those kids down our dirt road

Believe our mother would never
Imagine us capable of "telling stories"
Feel her questioning like a pneumatic drill
See her blanch at our boldfaced fibs
Her face pinched in wonderment—
How have I failed?

Flies caught in strips of sticky paper
We imprison ourselves in our false voices

A patient archeologist, mother sculpts truth
Through layers of falsehoods
Her horrified countenance registers
Our resolute dishonesty
Her motherhood trembles at our stone faces
The stubborn timbre, our brass lies

The Rabbit Trap

I am the child who
Trips the homemade door
The rabbit trap daddy made
To catch our wild supper

Cramped retreat shaped
Like a mailbox
Wooden prison where I crawl
Inside hide
Try to escape Mother's cajoling song

> *You always have your nose in a book*
> *You don't pay attention to how you look*
> *You need to fix your hair*
> *You always put things off to the last minute*
> *You're going to have a bottom big*
> *As your grandmother Gilliam's*
> *You're so smart you scare me*
> *Smarty smarty had a party and no one came but*
> *Little Miss Smarty*
> *If you do that you'll put me and your daddy in the graveyard*

The rabbit trap place I run to
From the stranger in my mother's eyes

Head bowed between my knees
Splinters in my back/fur all over

Weep for the Child, the Mother

On the river called Sorrow
A white boat sails
Assures the safety of Lucy, the Mother

Little Girl, a woman now
waves to her mother
Her ears, eyes—all senses open
free to find languages
for her experiences
free to leave her mother's beloved body
the unimaginable, imagined dark grave

Mother and Child separate
know understanding is
movement from self to the Beloved
that blessed union—
and return to self again

Two adults, lovers
and certainly friends
honor the liberated child
in each other—
bridge the River Bliss

Adolescence

Man in the Woods

I was thirteen and on my way to piano lessons…I have been taking lessons a year now, the toothless space in my mouth, proof I knew I was not good at playing the piano…I had talked the dentist, Dr. Carroll, if not my mother, into believing the pain in my fourth tooth, lower left, and he had pulled the sound tooth, which rescued me from the piano recital that first year.

That's not really how the story starts—actually the story comes from several directions at once—and converges on a small road entering a woods.

Another way to enter this story would be…"The pig hung wide open in the entrance to the hayloft in my father's barn." A false foreshadowing, but a graphic backdrop to my emerging girlhood. I was stunned and ashamed for that sow, so irreverently sprung to our sight in the morning of her hushed domestic slaughter. I avoided the barn, but I have not forgotten the impression of her mute signal, her violent solo.

The problem with taking piano lessons seemed to be a disconnection between my head and my hands. I knew the source of that clunk which I heard in the pauses, played by my forced fingers, but I was not telling…

I was walking to Mrs. Jones's house that March or November, this late afternoon—knowing full well I had not practiced and would have to fake it, knowing this was another link in a long line of false notes, knowing the piano was not my springboard to fame beyond these hills.

The day's light was copper/burnished/bright on brown leaves either leftover from winter or late fall leaves/moist/unfrostbitten…I don't remember what season it was—either early spring or late fall, before summer or before winter—maybe March or November…but for me, my body, *it was spring*—life bubbling through me all senses wide open, except for my brain momentarily fogged at the thought of thirty minutes of uncertain notes, tinged with violence.

Eyelids lowered, I glanced down my body—breasts like young corn nubbins, my mother would throw out husking corn for creaming. I liked my knees…

ever' now and then, I'd lift my dress to look at my knees admiring the smooth, supple slope inside my knee where my upper leg connected. I was walking the old highway so I was discreet in my gesture of admiration, seeing in my mind's eye/the shadow of a bending girl looking at herself slender, plump but skinny—on this curving country road avoiding the occasional car.

There was little color, less sound as I made my way, dreamily, along the roadside…it had been a good day at school. I was smart and that knowledge purred inside my head. I was pretty good at basketball. The highest jumper. So I was center for our team. I loved to wear navy blue or white shorts, sports, the only place this was allowed except in our backyard. Wearing shorts, my legs leapt. I knew I had good legs—my hair, my face another story, I had cute feet too. I used to wake up Saturday mornings and lie gingerly in bed wafted by the remains of old sleep—looking at my feet. They were slender, the toes proportionate, but individual. I pretended the toes were people. We cuddled each other. It was a good feeling playing with my feet…I could remember my sister and me lying feet forward to each other, our toes curled into that unmentionable part of the other one's small body, giving each other good feelings…

I can't remember the names of the people who lived down the road that led into the oak woods. That road was unwalked by me. My mother said not to go down that road—ever. I had just passed it today, my body aroused as always by its unknown, a natural invitation to explore. To escape the metronomical steps to sit, straight as an unsharpened pencil, beside Mrs. Jones's expansive bottom on the bench in front of her Baldwin.

This afternoon a voice called after me: *Do you want to fuck*, a man's voice, not quiet like mine this moment—but loud and clear—*DO YOU WANT TO FUH-UK*, he called—words from the woods, no man in sight.

Between my legs a small trickle of feeling lifted to that word—a thread of feeling within my body speaking to my mind—my body lifted its small heads, small flowered umbrellas of desire—flowers flickering into flame.

The second split and my mother's words crashed down on my head: *what kind of man would yell that in front of an ignorant girl—a monster of a man—a monster.*

But the tones to me had been velvet...a green scum of a creature with mossy green bulges...The sensations of *yes, yes, yes,* echoing my young body.

(Years later, I mused, "I can't remember any sexual feelings between age eight and eighteen.")

...*Run,* my voice ordered quietly through my legs. Running away / *like crazy* / I ran all the way/almost to the end of my breath, pain jogging my ribtracks, my feet hammering the red clay path through the hedge, into Mrs. Jones's house, terrified—not ready—arriving too excited for a piano lesson.

The wedge which slipped that day between my hands and head was simply this: I knew I had wanted to feel myself in those woods against that voice, know that word. I had wanted to follow my body, its tips—nose-tip, finger-tips, toe-tips, breast-tips, lip-tips, tongue-tip—my body eager for hidden pleasures spreading like peacock feathers' full colors in my brain, off the top of my head, between my legs.

Years later in a dream...I am entering a museum...I am a woman. I hear dream music/this is a dream museum—I, woman, climb the museum stairs. I am following the music I am making. I see a man in the museum rotunda — a statue of a man sculpted from electric gold or is it copper, bronze? Currents invisible emanate from his body, radiate...my feelings rise/open with pleasure/I am a woman I hear dream music/this is a dream museum. I climb the man's mountain. I hold his heartbeat in my hand. I follow the music I am making...

That night, my piano lesson finally over, I walked home on the same side of the road as I had come—away from the woods side—but I was secretly singing a little song...*man in the wooooooods, where are you, man in the woods, I'm here-ear...man in the woo...ooods.*

It would be years before I would know how to bring this story into sound:
the story ends in a trio of lines

That man in the woods is not a monster
That man in the woods . . . is me

I am the man in the woods.

She Sang Alto in the Church Choir

She sang alto
in the church choir
when I look at her
my ears burn
red as her crimson car coat
belted at the waist
with its mother-of-pearl, big buttons

Although I can't sing—
my voice carries the notes
I join the choir
What a friend we have in Jesus
All our sins and griefs to bare
hymn we sing at Sunday
morning worship service

At Wednesday night prayer meeting
I sit next to her
my cheeks on fire
while the preacher holds up hell
I fantasize heaven

The prickly feelings in my lap
wipe out the sermon
the wages of Sin is Death

I'm a girl—just turned fifteen —
she's everything I'm not;
she's beautiful, feminine,
sensuous, a secretary
she owns her own car—
Chevrolet Impala, Windsor blue

Her Auburn hair, golden-streaked
and bouncy
curves curly around her face
lights up her hazel eyes

I'm too shy to speak to her
my friend hands her a note
signed with my pseudonym—
I tell her I admire her—
Ask her, *Will you write to me?*
Tell her to put her answer
in the Suggestion Box
behind the door above the basement stairs
in the church vestibule

Wednesday night before
prayer meeting
I find the envelope Wedgewood Blue
Her handwriting is oval—
sloping like a kindergarten teacher's

I write to her about
playing basketball, about boys—
Carroll Lingerfelt and
Richard Whisnaut

She writes back about work,
the men she's dating—the
insurance man, the minister—
finds fault with each of them

I hide my identity—
she pretends not to know
my notes hide my crush on her
But when I am a national winner
for my Farm & Home Electric
project, she congratulates me

I am the subject of an
editorial in the *Citizen and Times*
Asheville, NC, newspaper 1952.

Blue-eyed girl, named after her father
helps him dig locust post
holes, wire electric fence
around family farm
wins Westinghouse scholarship—
first time national winner is a girl

During prayer meeting our hands touch
holding the hymnal
As we sit down she whispers
"You send me"

That summer Daddy and Mother
are delegates to the Wesleyan Church
Conference in Indiana—
they'll be gone a whole week
I beg them to get Meg Brittain
to stay with me

We sleep together—
sometime within the night
I awake, see the moonlight
southern, soft lay its cheek
against her breast. I hold my breath
Is she asleep or is she playing possum?

I dream we make a home together
in the mountains a secluded cave
sheltered by smoky blue ridges

Altar Call

The preacher closes his sermon
His voice climaxes with the invitation—
Is there someone here tonight
Who feels the hand of Jesus on her shoulder?
Someone whose life is burdened with sin?
Won't you come forward and give your life to Jesus,
Ask Him to come into your heart—
Be washed by His precious blood?

Brothers and sisters can you feel the presence
Of the Holy Ghost?
Sister Knupp, will you please
Play a few more verses (as we bow our heads in prayer)
"Just As I Am Without One Plea"—softly, gently
The hymn stirs the souls in the congregation.

The young girl's body is aroused
The music caresses like an imagined lover.
A wave of desire to be good
Eases her embarrassment.
Resolved, the sinner leaves the pew,
Her cheeks burning,
She kneels at the altar railing,
Head in her arms.
The pastor and the devout gather 'round
Lay hands on her young body and pray.

The "carnal man" inside her is stubborn as a pine knot.
Penitent, yes, but she wants to hold onto herself:
Cannot form the words to invite Jesus in.

The preacher works up a saintly sweat.
The gathered saints hold up
The lost soul to "The Throne of Grace."
Sunshine spreads slowly across her face;
Her willful black heart is transformed,
Washed in the blood of the lamb.
Redeemed, she stands up and testifies,
"Thank you, Jesus, for forgiving me
For hitting my sister—
Until the next time."

The Carnal Man

Wesleyan Methodism's carnal man
lives inside her/my plump body

what I would not do, I do
what I would do, I don't

her body is ripe
open to God knows what

girlchild's legs squeezed close
sprawls on the living room floor

in another room her mother
pedals the sewing machine

she explores her peony bud
not too young to know the name for it

A warmth flares pleasure
then embarrassment her mother
says—*You'll end up in Morganton*
if you touch yourself

years later a sophomore up North
at Houghton College she will remember,
in Colonial American Literature,
Puritan Jonathan William's Sermon—
"Sinners in the Hands of An Angry God"—
her mother.

Note: "Morganton" refers to a mental institution.

Untitled

Ganano Nesbitt sat next to me in algebra, the wall seat. She was attractive, popular outside of class; in the class she was very quite, almost sullen. She never raised her hand, and when inevitably Miss Mitchell called on her she paled instead of blushed. Her skin was dark, her hair darker, like an Indian's. Other classmates looked on my paper to see what answer I had got—she never did. She put her papers folded into her book and closed it before the class was over. The last week of school she did not come to class. I don't remember noticing her empty seat. But I've never forgotten the dull thud in my mind when I heard she had killed herself.

She had gone home from school, they said, and walked on down to the country store. She bought a Sunbeam white layer cake with white icing — that's all—and had stood in the slant-eyed rays of the afternoon sun. Just outside the screen door. She stood there and ate the whole cake, bite after slow bite.

Then she hanged herself in her backyard in the apple tree.

I rode my bicycle down Sand Hill School Road the next afternoon after school. The circles my feet pushed were deliberate. I was going to ride my bike to the dead girl's house.

The tree stood off the old highway visible from the road breathtakingly beautiful in a burst of apple blossoms. The swing rope remained.

I stood straddling my blue bike, a girl also fifteen, looking to see the slit in that blue air that opens into void.

I will grow up to be a writer and I will write about this, I felt in the small of my back. I will hear the silence speak—I will try to figure out how the magnetism, the electric buzz of this mountain May day did not hold her...how could this aura aromaed in pink turn sour in a young girl's mouth? The buds of a fruit tree appear jagged-edged like broken glass in her coal-black eyes? What tenterhooks inside her pained her toward that last act?

I went on to the corner country store, source of the words about her last moments alive. I entered and restepped the steps…over to the bakery rack… out the screen door…standing in the beaten hot red clay store yard, I felt alone.

My bicycle carried me quickly the three miles across the boundary I had violated. I could not get my mind off what had happened.

Ganano was to be buried in the cemetery tomorrow. I had just passed it and I had seen the grave had been dug. That opening lay alongside the dug dirt/silent/nothing in that community that day registered violence…nothing but my mind straining at windmills, real revolutions, emotions barely born in me eager for experience…dying to know…

I probed what I knew like a tongue in a just-pulled tooth; she had left a note directing that her funeral be held in the high school auditorium. She had picked the most good looking and popular boys in the school to be her pallbearers. And her plans were being followed—it was the least they could do.

I made the hill and coasted home, shaken to my very bones.

Must be she couldn't imagine another day…like she was.

Miss Bouge and Miss Bell

Two old maids
Petite Miss Bouge and stout Miss Belle
One elegant / the other irascible
Live together in a Victorian house
In Asheville, North Carolina, on Cumberland Avenue

Eight hanging ferns
Greet the visitor
In the oval arches of the wider-than-wide veranda
Potted germaniums line the front steps

Miss Bell opens the heavy oak door
I am invited to tea
She offers a brusque grace
As we enter the genuine parlor

I feel a sense of being chosen
Quietly identified to enter
Their inner world—art on the walls
Books in bookcases
Bric-a-brac
Comfortable wicker furniture

Interest shown in me, the tomboy

Next time Miss Bouge and Miss Bell
Will invite me to lunch in a restaurant
Acknowledge my graduation early from high school
They write me a check for college textbooks

And then Miss Bouge says, "Miss Belle and I want to pass
Down to you our silver gravy ladle engraved with rose clusters,
A family heirloom"

They did not know how like them
I would come to be.

Dawn in a Dream's Eye

—orangepink light gone not a minute later—changes/into yellow spreading light/bleached white

I play Hide-and-Go-Seek. I am It. I
Burrow my forehead into the oakbark…67,
68, 69. *Ready?* I call. A sweet silence
Answers. Light shifts shapes through
The seam of Night. Land's edge. Clear
As outline the black hulk plods wild the
Blueing sky.

I am looking for Dixie…behind the stump
Pile.

When the Bear picks me up and heads for
The pasture, the smell of honey widens
My forehead. I dig my fingers shivering
Into the small of its back—careful
Not to caress the fur the wrong way.
The black body furs beneath my hands.

The Bear lifts me across the barbed wire
Electric fence—ignores the pasture
Gate. One or two locust posts like
Ancient missiles give up their ground,
Their zigzag ranks, in the wake of the
Thrust. Grass and clover crush. A long
Low sound clears the Bear's throat.

Grief inside bursts like a sneeze

Hey Bear, I say, *Hey Bear.*

The Gun Scene

I lay awake in the dark under the quilts. In the moonlight turning slightly I could see a curl of my sister's hair asleep within the indentation of her neck—that was my place to give her sugar, meaning that's where she would let me kiss her, a sister's self-conscious kiss. "I love that little curl," I thought, "that neck, even that sister"...I stretched my eight-year-old self enjoying the elastic tension at the end of a soft dream—feeling my toes reaching for my growth between the sheets which were cold beyond where my feet had been. I snuggled my nose into my sister's soundly asleep back; at the same time my body said, "Before you get back to sleep—you have to get up and go to the bathroom." Buttermilk —it was that other glass of buttermilk sending me out of bed. The commode was white-cold but bearable as I looked full-face into the moon, windowed at the end of the tiny bathroom.

On my way back to bed to shyly steal heat from Joann (across the line she had drawn down the middle of the bed) I saw a line of light under the kitchen door—a wide yellow line like a mistake somebody made in art drawing a brown door without a bottom line. Doors were never shut (except my daddy's and mother's bedroom door on Sunday afternoons after church, after Sunday dinner, after the dishes were put away). The little house was too small for shut doors. The kitchen, the largest room in the house, had a door but it was never shut.

I stopped.

I could hear the voices of mother and daddy wrestling...I opened the door...to see...I can't say what I saw. Trying to know what happened... in that kitchen...my father was lifting the refrigerator to throw it out the back door. He looked like he was going to crush my mother against the kitchen sink on his way to hurl it off the high back porch.

I stood there unnoticed on the linoleum floor memorizing the swirls of the pattern trying not to...

"Uh", I spoke up. "Uh, uh, uh I'M HERE." My words were swept up in my mother's

"GO GET THE GUN"

Within the gun scene I took the part of my mother. After it was all over, my father, no doubt resheathed the gun in its brown burlap cover taking it back leaning it in its place. It was my mother's side I went to.

In her anguish she pulled me to her. She pressed her face into my small body and poured her grief into me filling the tiny quivering cups at the ends of all my nerves. Her grief was that she had come to this: the need, sob, (more sobs)—worse—*the impulse to shoot her husband.* And I sided with her because her suffering was greater, was my own...child not knowing I was already moving toward the day I would understand her—my mother, my child.

I loved "my daddy"—*my daddy* let me go down into the dirt basement with him to help him skin a rabbit. He told me to insert my two fingers under the furry skin and pull when he said "pull." First, he slit the skin, a straight line across the stomach. The smell burst forth—I turned my nose away and I held on for dear life. He pulled the skin over the head. That was the hardest part. I was glad he had the head end.

I was the apple of his eye. That I was not a son had come not to matter.

He was the apple of my eye, too. My mother fought for him; my mother fought me; my mother fought him.

The word *lover* held no power for me then. But I was caught by their love. Her virginity no longer possible, his male organ no longer fantasy. I, the child, the proof. My mother feeling God knows what, feeling powerless... feeling powerless...went for the gun...she threatened to kill him, moving toward him...but as she neared...she stopped...was it his body (that fire between them/flintmade) that stopped her—or did I?

Had I gone for the gun, my daddy's gun, he used for hunting rabbits, squirrels for us to eat? The gun propped in the closet in their bedroom in the narrow space to the left inside their bedroom closet door. It's hard to remember.

The realization of her failure to shoot him spread over her like goosebumps before a faint—she turned the gun on me to wipe me out in one trigger.

What stopped her—all I know is some nights alone at that place between fall and winter I see the August sounds of katydids frozen and I hear a silence louder than the discharge of a gun.

All I know is inside me, terror—everything stopped.

Sometimes I don't even know if this story is true—it might could be a fantasy. But I can smell terror—a metallic smell—a gun in my face, small black moon/full/looking me in the eye.

Whatever in him/between them—drove her to that aborted action—that ultimate humiliation? He had mastered her—for the remainder of their lives which have been long—this happened thirty-seven years ago—except in the small atomic clusters of her spreading rebellion, *Don't tell your Daddy,* through which her life has turned.

But my daddy had paid dear—his blond, curly-headed, blue-eyed little girl had turned against "the night mother lost her mind." I rebelled against the BODY I imagined had evoked such violence.

I blamed my daddy, and my mother never told me any different.

The next day they both acted as if it didn't happen.

I went to school, cried in and out of classes. I knew nothing would ever be the same. But there were no words with which to tell my teachers—just eight years old—red-rimmed eyes rubbed redder by the end of the day.

After that I went to my father from time to time for the Rite of Touch which I initiated: *"Goodnight Daddy / Sweet Dreams / I Love You."*

One afternoon years later / grown in my forties at the airport saying goodbye to him my lips seeking his cheek I involuntarily sobbed outloud and looked around and hoped no one heard.

I remember tonight / looking back / that I held my mother many times—perhaps I held her that night, Horror's head on Terror's lap. . .Later I fled under the covers in my bed where I tried to disappear. Where I held my breath. Where I wanted to die.

To punish them? NO—to punish myself—to leave a flawed life, earth forever marred by the blood of imagination.

Love

Burning Flowers

when *is* changes to *was*
the real pain comes
sharp
in the image of flowers burning

mourning is active
the whole body lifted
full trigger
the movement of grief

sadness the sweet supple
blanket comes after

there are women
who burn
unnamed by any revolution
women who simply turn
in the image of bodies burning
in love
unclaimed
except by air

Alone, the Garden Comes to Me

for you, beloved Susan

alone, the garden comes to me
last night's forty-four evening primroses
a sweet symphony of spiral buds
light-infused trip an invisible pulse
quietly releases a troupe of golden-skirted dancers
each her own opening on divine cue

alone, the garden comes to me
this morning brings limp-bosomed blossoms
at rest taking a breath
a cool wet dawn where cardinals court
dew shyly disappears in the grass
at the bird bath gold finches flirt
a doe, tail flicking, calls her fawn into the woods
a bobcat hunkers down up a summer hill

a resonating day at hand
all mine
and for you, too

love, jimmie

P.S.—Susan, Kathleen says that the bumper crop of primroses are from
your garden here.

Paris/in my mind's/eye

green pinpoints
the air charged with light
puddled by rain
your eyes
refracted
held by mine
along the Seine

Poem for Rita

irish eyes
open
rain through
human eyes
land's expansive
smile
focus in human
flesh
wit's thorn
compassion's rose

The risk of relationship is what one comes to know
about the other juxtaposed to what one comes to know about one's self

Style

no one talks about
the placenta of death

I want to go
engulfed by your skin

until the first startled cry
after my last breath

Seawild

I stand on the head of a pin
trying to embrace
the ocean
with my flailing arms
The song of your voice
enters my longing
over and over
the sky settles over
me/rehearses the waves
crash within crash

rocks, spume, shell
waterfly

The Fear Poem

Fear
Comes
Like an intruder
Unannounced
It screams through the reach of the doorbell
Or jerks me out
Of bed
With its hard black plastic
Telephone receiver hands lift off
Ripping my eardrums out
My ears
Leaving them dangling ducts
At the ends of molten brain-grains
Or memory   half rock/senseless sands
Caught in the sieves of my selves
Struggling for the gold that is me
Mine

Fear forces open
Apart
The unnamed lips between my legs
Inserts the knife eagerly
To cut through

Leftover umbilical cords
At last   to expose   the
Eye of the boil
Stringed to assert its yellow head
To lift off the scab lid
Of first wounds
In the end to leave
The quickening quaking at
The center   the quick
Where child/mother   cleave
To depart   one the other

Welcome fear I come to meet you
Lick the intricacies of my ribs
Caress my lung cage that
Holds my life captive
Take my breath
Plug up my ears with your
Cotton gauzy smell
Two fingers the spaces over my nose
Swallow my exposed eyes that wanly
Roll behind inadequate skinfilms
Tongue them off their unconscious axis
Then thrust your own
Voices prong into the
Longing channel that
Begins at my mouth
And probing push to
Meet the knife's point
Fear I whisper
I want to destroy
Myself
Against your blank wall
It is you who are my fear
Your eyes pull mine
To touch the luminous
Orbs of your own seas
Whose roads
Go to the ultimate blackness/eventually
Your fingers rest waiting
To mix with mine
Fear's blind winding wine
While
Above the wishbone of

Your pelvic cave beneath your breasts
Protrudes your belly
Pushing towards mine
To greet the convoluting
Dead stump center
Of stagnant umbilical cords ponded
Gordian knotted
And needled together
Your legs cradle with mine
In the rocking motion
Of children   severed
Alone
Perpetually moved by a fear
That will   can never   be
Named
Only known
My fear   I love you
Gently now   lean
Against the rag-edge arm
Of my caring
And cry into me
Your moisture   winter spring summer
Fall
Rainburn
And together we will reach
        The full sheathing
Of a harvest
That is not premature.

Woman/Mountain

you empty my words
tongues/streams underground
give home to baby rivers
mountains reach for mount'ins

I am sky to your dream

earth/hand turns me into flower
rock breaks into fire
smoke of cloud breathes the coves
flame leaps the ridge
blue/mountain/ruby red
external explosion

original abstract scene

Where the Poem Comes From

On hold on the
telephone, while my
lover takes a business
call in New Jersey
at work—*for a
long time*—early
in our relationship

"Lover, face
yourself."

As I write this poem upstairs
the sun strikes the brass bed
I see it is in the acceptance
of my loud longing
that I can celebrate
your independence and freedom

I see it is in my embrace
of my quivering heart that
I can take mine...

Untitled

within the skin of your back
night after night
while you fall into sleep's sealed canyon

my fingertips, my hand palms
move your muscles
end of the day
love clay in my hands

replay the tiny fingered
touch of the skin of my
mother's breasts

As I unconsciously mirror in nerve endings
the feel of her skin
shyly I trace the prickly
feeling over your side over
the slopes of your breasts
around your nipples
Tell you how light finds
our home places

Invitation to the New Decade

for Geri Elizabeth

feel my upper lip on your lips—
lower lips
nothing touches
me like my mouth
there
or your mouth there
come meet me
at the iron gate
our passion

untitled

we go
across our threshold
desire, i am here
love is together
dream, you've come home

Two Stanzas from a Long Love Poem

I.
you call me slowly down
corridors of desire

i come to you

my eyes balanced for the first time
on a stem
of clear blue

2.
i see
light as feathered light
circle within arms
whole as one
without fear

Today I Uncovered the Violets

Today I uncovered the violets
yesterday I wrestled
fantasy's angel
a knot in the cloth of my life
I faced the face of panic
stilled her hysterical tongue
sweeping the scarred wooden floors
did not lie down
washed the dishes made food
picked the litter along the hedges
wrote overdue letters
swallowing guilt
answered a poem
lived in relation to the children
their doll boyfriends
talk that will never include me
but grows in my house
which did not fall during the winter
while I record the poem
ducks eat our bread
beneath the bedroom window
emotion is energy
will move me when the fuel is gone
the sun over
this spring is different
you are still here
and I held true

today I uncovered the violets
love made me

Missing You

being real
was my homage to you
and then I hid away
as unreal as willingly hidden
as I could be.

You are seen
by few.
Bits and pieces

I am waiting for your hand
to walk me out of the trees

dear one, Canadian geese linger
non-communicative nonsense to me
they are boisterous with their own kind

clearly setting themselves apart
but I am circling this pond alone
slanted down the green tunnel path

the promise of rest, shore and a ride home
just beyond.

let's make love
a priority
my oboe calls
out to your horn

Meadow River

The feelings I first had for you—
      when we met at your mother's house
      amaze my memory

      what my daddy said he felt
      when he first met my mother

How could emotion leap the line of gender
      I did not stop to ask—

          "I want to take you home to my brass bed"
          is what I said

It takes a decade before you come to lie there—
      my exhausted guest—

      you bring your book on celibacy
      I read to you H. D.
      while you quietly drop off to sleep

The weekend over that Sunday afternoon before you leave—
      you kiss me
      the middle of my upper lip
      kissing me warm breathing kisses
      until you reach the corner —

      longing lines my throat
      my breath turns over in my mouth

For thirty-two years now we've made our love
into a meadow river.

Love Poem

Your mouth teaches me
The double entendre of lips
Your body unfolds me
Which tongue is mine?

You call from the ocean's edge
Nothing keeps me from spilling at your mouth's door
We make love—
The fortunate plays
The cricks in our necks
Our backs ache
The shared limbs/the after spooning

How more possible the world seems

You make visible the long love—
Our anxieties, hopes and fatigues
Surrender the partnership of flesh

Your sure wave breaks over me
Emotion's skies open
Wet as umbrellas
We arrive shaken inside our doorway
In the place we've made home
Lover's hollows and curves fill
One body drapes the night dream's edge

Housework

writing my story
I set out
like Don Quixote
but not like him
my horse is my house
I ride it as it moves
over the crack in the basement
Above the stream underneath.
It is as broken as Rocinante.

I touch pen to paper
10:42 p.m./temp. 37°
April 17, 1978
Mill Street
"Tonight it rains.
A spring cleaning rain
—not warm really
but warm in Buffalo
the pressure behind my
left eye lessens.
I sense a blocked dam
of blood pushing"
This writer sets out

I move out of
The block in my brain
within my
head which cuts
me off
I write new arteries
which flow toward
actions I have not taken
The Quest:
I write my body

...I dreamed as recent as last night I sent
a stream of fishes all colors into the ocean:
I spun them endlessly as a simple web
thrust/for the beauty of it. I felt the
power of making water images into real fish.

12:44 p.m./50°
April 18, 1978

Suspension Bridge

We are in too high heights
the bridge we want to swing
sways mile high
like the one at Grandfather's Mountain
in Carolina

our imaginations thrust
pilings plied earth deep
earth aches
the steel structure rises
loudly mirrors light
snaps silent

the span is reached
twin rivulets of metal touch

the innocent river slides underneath

the mountain bed receives the press
the joined fire

the lovers   eyes averted
walk on water
walk on air

Fall, Raking Leaves

(for Geri—author of my happiness)

we hold the dead
up with our lives
dead branch lies
horizontal in the tree of heaven
back yard tree
at the border
the dead remind us where
not to hurry to go
we are the only body
that they have

Beloved

Beloved
you are poem
to my life
simile, metaphor
heartbeat
weaving, form

we fall asleep
lips upon lips
our breath
indistinguishable

flesh listens
while we lie safe
in sleep
your hand
rests around my neck
light as
wing tips
your hands breathe
belief

Flesh Made Word

(for my lover)

My body bows upward
Lifts to meet the firm
Light, flickering motion
My lover's tongue
Awakens hooded rosebud
Eros' eye

Your tongue evokes purple cloudbursts
What Emily Dickinson images
White ropes/loops uncoiling between her and Sue
Close in New England's 19th century woods
A women's rendezvous

Tongue a solo of limbs
You move rhythm and myth
Fern tip leads me up a precipice
Muscles pulled half-moon
Maidenhead circled

I begin the long climb
Up Melancholy Mountain/through Denial Pass
My body taut as a drum skin plays dumb
An audible prayer/*Don't stop Don't stop*

A silence mimics death
Involuntary now like a sneeze
I receive the word
From the unwavering flame
Your faithful tongue

Night Poem

"A claim of life wakes to the life in the other"

...the warmth of your body
   drew our lives into rich contouring/our fire
   over and over
   there is no poem you have to make
   we are alive
   a poem is a burial   NO.
   the poem is the empty tomb
   it is our bodies shared light
   in the dark
   that is not the same/alone
...the warmth of my body

Confidence

pain holds me like a paper clip
within the city
you are everywhere
in places where
we were
in Jennifer's emotions

the lighthouse
somewhere
dumb

I am your lover
your body fluid in memory
envelopes me

the wind comforts my skin

to turn love into art
I make the poem

I hold off pain
like building the fire
wards off the April animals

I am the wild animal

in rage
love flames
in this poem
desperate
to affirm
Eros as earth

I am your lover

I will not avoid
my feelings

I grasp death by the hands
take the knife
slit my throat/cut out
the voice that did not hold you

I live

you rise
in me
bejeweled by real tears
a gown I give you
in my dream

weaver of fantasy

child's play:
  red rover, red rover
  let my lover come over

my arms hold
my self unsplit

Alone in this intelligent body
my heart's mouth hungry
for every scrap of evidence
we loved as lovers

I am your lover
Lautrec in every corner does not move
me like the memory of you
intent in your work
moving toward the moment
in bed on the deep deep-blue sheets
where you lie whole
having made love with me
I watch the light enter the curls of your hair
Light that caresses me with memory
of where/we formed/together

I will see lovely forever
the Light

You were my lover
Art celebrates the image that lasts
but Love is endless motion

Away from you
these rhythms
lash me
removing my cells

I enter silence with resolve
I write:
"The first time we make love is as good as any last"

"I am the Lover" break the words
I CAN'T STAND THIS weeps the Dream

I want you
As we will continue to be
in my relentless imagination

Beyond the poem
the final act: to love
to encircle the lovers.

I am your lover
our love lies a light-sailed harbor
where balloons lift simple as birds
a shuttered eye

Jennifer Margaret

Jennifer Margaret
you draw thirteen rabbits
doing thirteen different things
you say, "Food is a kiss to my stomach"
when you are three
you will not eat a broken cookie
after your first day of school
you announce you're never going back

you jump the longest jump
you win trophies for running
when I was bed depressed
you brought me plastic flowers
you said they won't ever die
you love animals
one summer you and I touch
treebark, moss, leaves, grass, flowers
I set you and your sister down
over the log into a wasp's nest
I carry you both out of the woods
you scream bloody murder

we go through the white waters
your adolescence/our rafts collide
but we earn each other's love
crest of the wave your name means
in you life is a blonde art

Daughter

Daughter
in Marea Jill the diamond
breaks into stream
imagination
the blood jet
you give
yourself like pieces of bread
pages of poem

to be friend
to be friend to me
but we are daughter/mother
who is the child
lines blur
the heart breaks
clear I am me
clear you are you
in your own words
"solid as stone/fragile as glass"

you take yourself
to the line
between horizons
(I the uninvited guest)

your body holds

a vulnerable strength
pulses
Kilauea
volcano to the sea
fire meets water

Across Time

Doris S. Payne

1933–1970

probable
cause of death
crucified by the
sexual mores of
American society.

Cemetery: Mount Tabor, Virginia

Trespasser

The trespasser is no less awed
   by the beauty
         he can not
         possess
and still be a trespasser.

Bandit

death came and lay on our front porch
and wagged its tail
and we patted its head and gave it water

the dog puppy came and took and left
leaving this ache inside of us, wagging.

On Writing

Time stands still
in the eye of writing storm

no wonder we struggle
so hard to get there

if it were easy
we might never come back

Wait

wait these are not your names
wet with imagination
my heart blurs/fails
who are you

we are your other
brother the sister
who is other

our molecules circle
the same/different dance—

that circle in the night
outside Charlotte
that frightened you
that you never forgot that terrified you who
did not know her past, her whirling own self.

A Cancerous Eros

Uncle Ed brags
"My Daddy's daddy owned
Twenty-one slaves"

He gets thrown in the brig
In Newport News, Virginia
For baiting colored soldiers with epithets

His discharge from the Navy
During World War II is dishonorable
But he shows no shame
Unfurling the grey-black flag, his mania
Bias incessant talking, chain-smoking

He has been high school educated only
But his mechanical genius
Lands him a good job
Working on the atomic bomb
In Oak Ridge, Tennessee

He shows me a sizable picture
The men on his shift
(*They've all died a cancer so far*
'cept me and Bruce Gaddy
and Troy Fletcher)

When his cancer is diagnosed
His estranged wife, Aunt May,
Who is part Cherokee
Who has listened to his disparaging
Her Native American culture
Who finally had left him
Returns to care for Uncle Ed

Angry that she won't have sex
One Saturday night
He holds her hostage and naked
Until she slips away nude
Sunday morning into the neighborhood
Tells on him, his sorry story

Alone in his frustration
Uncle Ed shoots himself
In the genitals
Drives himself to Veterans' Hospital

Then he calls me, his niece
On the telephone
"I shot my God damn balls off"

I visit my uncle at the Oteen Hospital
(My uncle who with Aunt May
used to babysit my little sister,
my cousin, Beverly, and me)
It was Uncle Ed who taught me,
A six-year-old, how to make a fist
Aim at our spoiled brat of a three-year-old cousin, Beverly's chin
Do it just right there
(Showing me the spot at the side of my own chin)
and you'll deck 'er.

An Apology

Genuine human change is one to one.

—Jung

I've known your names since before Daddy died. He and Jill and I drive down Old Fort Mountain to go to church at the Mt. Hebron Wesleyan church, where Mother's people are members. Mother's second cousin, Cassie Halford Burgin, is a member of the church. We are late. The service has started. They are singing, *Shall We Gather at the River.* Someone cordially hands us a hymnal. Daddy holds the book with less of a tremble than I imagined. Jill sings soprano to my alto. The preacher acknowledges us, asking that we introduce ourselves. "We are Lucy Gilliam's family," I say. "This is my father, Noland Gilliam. His mother was Joe Halford's girl, who grew up in the Bethelem community. I'm Jimmie Margaret, and this is my daughter, Jill."

"We're so happy to have you worship among us. Today we're having dinner on the grounds after the service, and there's plenty of food. We hope you'll stay and break bread with us."

I've known your names since that day, as we were heaping our plates with deviled eggs, bread and butter pickles, fried apples, runner beans, creamed corn, and southern fried chicken, Rebecca Knupp, Cassie's daughter, approached. "Jimmie Margaret, would you like to see the list of the names of the family slaves?"

No-one ever talked about the family owning slaves, that silent wound. But *I've known your names* since that day in 1986...*Our Slaves,* a list kept by the Burgins.

In 1903, Grandfather Gilliam inherited the Burgin's four hundred acres. James Gilliam sold land at the time of his marriage, at the birth of each child, at each family crisis. In 1926, he sold the last sixty acres. It's all gone.

The land was lost, but the hidden world of the slaveholder seeped into the 20th century. Whispers overheard:

The funny thing is, we took pride in our ownership. We were good to them. Some stayed on with us after emancipation, the War of Northern Aggression, the Great War.

In the land of the sky, the heavens reflect a truth that is hard to come by: Christianity was used to justify a superiority that separates the destinies of people by the color of their skin.

At the root of enslavement, a fatal flaw: the failure to imagine that there but for the grace go I/we.

What can I do with the list of the names of the slaves?

A silence centuries long blankets and suffocates.

Time is no excuse.

Great-granddaughter of slaveholders, I know it's impossible for me to know what you suffered, the devastation: your lives stolen, your true names obliterated, your families dissolved, broken up. But *I must give voice to your names.*

Jarred, born March 16, 1828

Silvey, born August 19, 1831

George Percy, born August 1832, died September 13, 1858

Grace Orindia, born October 13, 1855

Annabelle Barneth (Burgin), born October 28, 1831

Samuel B., born September 29, 1842

Lucinda B., born October 13, 1855

Isaac B., born October 28, 1831

Adolyphus B., born June 21, 1850

Edith Selina B., born October 7, 1851

Hannah Deliah B., born October 26, 1853

I must acknowledge my great-grandfather's legacy:

One Negro man named Cato, twenty-six years of age, willed to Alvey Burgin with two beds and other furniture, and two cows and calves.

One Negro girl named Dicey, about twenty-nine years of age, willed to Martha Burgin.

One Negro girl named Nancy, about twenty-seven years of age, willed to Leah Burgin.

One Negro man named Dick, about twenty years of age, willed to Robert Burgin.

One Negro man named Casias, about fifteen years of age, willed to Leah Burgin.

One Negro boy about twelve years of age, called Barnet, willed to John Burgin.

I am here now, and while I still have a voice, I want you to know the remorse and sadness I feel for the terrible violence done by my people, sometimes in the name of the Lord...

Mark an end to the denial, underline the grief and horror in our shared story. A genuine apology.

To speak aloud the names of the slaves, audible proof of the hidden wounds inflicted by the slaveholder on their descendants—and on his.

I am sorry, Jarred. I imagine your eyes fill with contempt as mine fill with tears.

I am sorry, Silvey. I reach out to take your hand. You roll your eyes and walk away.

I am sorry, Alexis, Charles, Lena.

I am sorry, Armacie, Brunetta, Alberta.

I am sorry, Cynthia, Marilyn and René.

Forgive me, Lorna, forgive me, René.

Jarred, Silvey, George Percy, Grace, Orindia, Annabel, Samuel, Isaac, Adolphus, Edith Selina, and Hannah Deliah, Cato, Dicey, Nancy, Dick, Casias, Barnet.

In the span of your births, I was form yet unborn, curled in the corner of an ancestor's imagination.

Words caught in the cloth of my rag throat, without voice, unable to move the dark bell in their deaf hearts, tolling

Wrong. Wrong. Wrong

until now / until now

you must never say history
repeats herself
spring says it new again

Graveside

I go to your grave, Mother
The car makes the hillside curve
At Pisgah View
Stops at the magnolia tree
I am alone
Your bones nudge the scab of my hidden tears
I weep within the rain
I walk up to your place sideways
As I once approached the Pacific Ocean
At Cape Disappointment, Oregon

I am your daughter on the way to the store
To buy cornmeal to fry okra
From Rhobena's garden

I have much to say to you, Mother
But now there is only time to arrange the silk flowers
Limp in the rain
I entwine two of them
One red, one pale purple
I do not tell you
Daddy has mowed down your lilacs
The rosebud bush

Your death still takes my legs away, Mother
But I walk on the air/my will
Away from the mirror you hold for me
Deep in the earth

I am your poet, Mother
Though my words do not grace your ears
I am bone of your bone
You stand in my frame
Bone catches in the throat
Of this grief

I became Poem
Having been called
Communist

The Artist

The glass in my feet is real
glass splinters of experience
I was never inclined
never took the time
did not know how
to see clearly

glass pieces; now drawn from
forming the small elephant
within my brain
I broke as a child

Locating My Uterus in the Universe

Written on the occasion of a massage soon after my hysterectomy,
which triggered grief from the loss, hearing poetry dancing in my
head.

a woman and her child
blocked by a broken wall
step over the rubble
into the bombed out edifice
red brick warehouse

rat fear freezes me
I surmise
she wouldn't take her daughter
in there
if there were rodents
shattered glass

I follow their stooping figures
crawl through a tunnel
which opens upon
a set of steps

a hundred footfalls
we descend
earthfloor beneath a sod ceiling

mother and daughter disappear

my women friends gather beside me
this is the closest
we'll ever come to knowing what it was
to be in the womb

a vast plain stretches before us
an underground ocean
water edges patterned like lace
wet the air with rhythm

Deathbed

You are sitting in your bed/pillows propped behind you
your back is straight/your eyes closed
your fingers intertwine
you wear a pink negligee/over the hospital gown
you have put lipstick on your thin lips
your cheeks are faintly rouged

the tall window to your right
takes in the evening light/diagonal across your breasts

you wait for me
daughter who lives up north
the one who had to have the last word

I say, *Hello lady*
walk the thousand miles/from your doorway to the bed
you take my hands/link my scared fingers
with your firm clasp

Put God first, you say
My heart is broken/for my family

What the Mountains Say

Cartwheel your childself
With sensory oblivion and live—
Not to tell the tale only but
To listen for the silent story

Before we were born
We were not mountains—
Not the Blue Ridge, the Great Smokies,
The Appalachians
We were invisible below earth's crust,
Molten and without voice

Three inland seas are shallow
Vast above our unimaginable peaks
Soft rains fall continuously
Silt and small stones and eroding ridges
Through millions of years build pressure
The seas' floor drops six miles
Crashes the earth's rim
Cataclysm

We rise up twenty-five-thousand feet
When the sound settles, hazy-blue and golden,
We are two hundred mountains—
Loam of your silence,
Home of your longing

I long to have you/call me by my name, Mother
my purse stuffed with poems
I do not read to you
instead I say, *I love you as deep as the universe*

What's bigger than the universe? you tease

You know what. . .my voice. . .is going. . .
you take a breath which catches/breath that never
breathes itself out

your eyes snap center/stare
I whisper in your ear, *Sweet dreams, Mother*
(words you used to tell us when you tucked us in)

you take with you   my voice

Editor's Note

Death arrives in its own time. And when it did, Jimmie's unfinished manuscript became the undertaking of the ones she left behind. Though she provided us with a clear outline for the organization of its themes, she did not finish every piece that she intended to include. In one notebook, I found an extensive draft on the names of pre-Civil War slaves owned by her family. Here, she asks what she could do with this list; how to break the long silence of their voices? "Time is no excuse," Jimmie writes, and she apologizes to each slave, speaking directly to them by their names, albeit those given to them by slave masters. When she exhausts that list, she continues on to apologize to their descendants, including some of her friends in the present day.

Though not polished or finished, this piece, "Apology" and many other poems titled "fragment," function seamlessly within the underlying theme of the book as a whole.

For what does it mean to be Torn from the ear of night?

When I put this question to Geraldine Grossman, Jimmie's life partner and wife, she replied:

"When Jimmie's mother died the line torn from the ear of night came to her. It felt like a ripping of a sort of loss in the night. Ear meaning our ability to listen to the earth, to nature to each other, our ability to hear life itself…the ear of night…it holds our dreams our fantasies, our vulnerabilities."

What centers the book is the writer's struggle with the contradictions between the normative, outer world—violent, destructive, and shaming—and her inner, emerging sexuality—sensual, rebellious, and deeply psychological. She must clench and tear fragments of her truth from the given, the woven cloth of land and ancestry. Jimmie transforms her inherited landscape—white Southern/Wesleyan Methodist/historic racism/homophobia—and gives voice to all that was forbidden. Grounded firmly in the land of the Blue Ridge Mountains, Jimmie slowly unravels family secrets and then rebuilds her life, weaving together something entirely new in the most intimate section of the book—"Love."

In "Love," we find ourselves among books, gardens, rivers, gravestones. Without pretense, Jimmie names the subject of her poems—daughters, lover, mother—the oppressive cloak of shame is discarded. Sexual pleasure is celebrated. Psychological healing demands truth and action. Jimmie knows that to delve into history risks coming back unrecognizable. From the poem "Wait" in the last section of the book, "Across Time":

> …the circle in the night
> outside Charlotte
> that frightened you
> that you never forgot that terrified you who
> did not know her past, her whirling self.

For Jimmie, it is more terrifying not to know one's past than to confront what frightens us. The stories in the section "Ancestry" are recalled like the scenes of a play. Dramatic, fragmented and with no resolution. We readers are left to re-imagine what happens next. In "Watermarks," we wish to save the desperate lovers the night they entered the "water-moccasined waters of Lake James." We cannot forget them and we are left to speculate how their fate might have differed. If only they had met at a time when it was not true that "Love is danger."

Jimmie never thought of herself as a prolific writer and yet the evidence is to the contrary. I found her writing scrawled across every possible at-hand surface—hotel notepads, airline napkins, index cards, invitations, torn envelopes, blank edges of newspapers, lined notebooks and random sheets of graph paper. I came to realize this preference for commonly found writing materials was integral to her writing process and easily overlooked in its chaotic state of handwritten notes.

This book includes many pieces that were previously published and undoubtedly familiar to anyone who has attended Jimmie's poetry readings. Although the untitled fragments that I discovered while leafing through her numerous piles of notes were not included in Jimmie's initial manuscript, I think they are concise, startling and congruous with the all the implications of meaning found in the title of the book.

As a portion of the book came from material that existed only in hand-written script, it is possible that I misread a word or two, and I cannot guarantee that Jimmie would have wholeheartedly agreed with my final edits on line-breaks. That said, I typed up the work in its found state as much as possible. I do not think Jimmie could have imagined how much *Torn* would increase in volume after Geri and I excavated piece after piece from her notebooks. My hope is she would be pleased with our choices and, at the very least, amused by our enthusiasm, respect, and love of her work.

For the past year, Jimmie's voice has sounded in my thoughts with every line of her work. It was a great comfort to grieve a friend and yet have that friend so present in the words of her poems, the slope of her handwriting. Geri Grossman and Debora Ott have generously shared this journey with me and I am forever grateful for their support with *Torn*, for their love and friendship.

Jimmie, though dearly missed, remains steadfast as our teacher. *Torn from The Ear of Night* is the map of a life that takes us to terrifying geographies and requires a brutal honesty from the author— "I carve the unspeakable words/on the child's cave wall/my mother's broken and I can't fix her."

In "Love," we are assured the price paid is rewarded. In the sexually explicit lines of "Flesh Made Word," Jimmie boldly claims her sexual identity, her right to be a sexual being; her desire to be with a woman:

> I begin the long climb
> Up Melancholy Mountain
> through Denial Pass/my body taut as a drum skin plays dumb
> an audible prayer
> *don't stop don't stop...*

Her courage as a poet challenges us to feel; to be honest; "To listen for the silent story."

As Jimmie would say, *Traveling mercies, dear reader.*

—Paula Paradise
November 1, 2016

Jimmie Margaret Gilliam

So many of the lives of women are buried by silence, a silence carefully hidden by layers of fear, anger, and shame, often within a self-imposed repression. I know beneath all those thick walls lies a passionate voice wanting to convert to life. If my poems can evoke the desire to open that expression, I will have fulfilled my own hope for my work in the world.

Although Jimmie Margaret Gilliam spent the majority of her life in the North, the South where she grew to young adulthood formed a large part of her identity. She never lost the traces of her Southern accent, and she treasured her "Little House," the home in which she grew up and to which she often returned throughout her life. Born into a deeply religious family in Asheville, North Carolina, on August 7, 1935, Jimmie spent her formative years in the Appalachian Mountains, where she came to see in her surroundings the truth of what she read in her Bible: There is beauty in everything.

She was a keen observer of not just nature's changing seasons but of the changes in her own life. *Ain't No Bears Out Tonight,* her 1984 memoir in prose poems of these years, spoke poignantly and with unusual openness and honesty of both a difficult family life and her earliest sexual awakenings. It was no doubt both her religious upbringing and the social mores of the times that directed those early urges toward young men.

Jimmie first arrived north of the Mason-Dixon Line to attend Houghton College, a small, Christian school about sixty-five miles southeast of Buffalo, New York. "North Carolina and Western New York made me the woman I am," Jimmie said. In keeping with both society's and her Southern family's expectations for her, Jimmie married after she graduated from Houghton in 1956 and found a teaching job at Starpoint High School, just outside of Buffalo. In 1963, she gave birth to her daughter, Jill, and in 1967, her second daughter, Jennifer, was born.

Jimmie taught English and Creative Writing at Starpoint High School from 1956–71. It was an era when teachers were supposed to be authoritarian and mold their students, but Jimmie would have none of that. She knew the importance of opening their young minds to the possibility in their own lives, and encouraged them to be their authentic selves. She was accused of being a Communist and, along with five other teachers, fired. Her students dedicated their yearbook to Jimmie that year. As the primary breadwinner in the family, losing her job had a severe impact. It was during these turbulent times that her marriage dissolved.

Leaving Starpoint marked a seismic shift in Jimmie's life. She had begun to take her writing seriously in 1968, and she received early support and encouragement in her writing from Just Buffalo founder Debora Ott, who, by asking her to do readings and workshop, opened the door to the possibilities in her life. She bought a copy of Lawrence Ferlinghetti's *Coney Island of the Mind*, which inspired many poems of social justice, isolation, and betrayal. In 1971, she embarked on a new position, professor of English Literature at Erie County Community College, where she would remain until her retirement in 1995.

In 1965, Jimmie met Geri Grossman, a businesswoman from New York City with whom, it would seem, she had little in common. Geri's mother, Rita Wilson, worked for Jimmie's then-husband at the University of Buffalo, and they frequently gave her rides home from work. Through Jimmie's friendship with Rita, she learned about the daughter she'd abandoned more than twenty years earlier and was contemplating meeting, which she soon did. Shortly after, she introduced Geri to Jimmie, and they soon became fast friends. "We have an affinity for each other," was how Jimmie described it. Their friendship grew deeper over a ten-year period, and, says Geri, "We saw ourselves joining our lives in complete and unconditional love, respect, and commitment...*evernow*, a word Jimmie created to mean 'forever,'—and that's exactly how we lived...evernow in life and now in death."

The more time Geri spent in Jimmie's hundred-year-old home in Williamsville, the more she realized that it was where she wanted to be: it was home. Compared to the chaos of life in New York City, Mill Street was an oasis of tranquility. Jimmie, of course, was the creator of that. "She slowed everything down," Geri has said. "She was able to hold still and take you in. She was nonjudgmental. You were free to be who you were." Finally, after ten years together, Geri quit her job, packed her things, and moved in with Jimmie.

A rich literary scene was burgeoning in Buffalo in the early '70s, and women's voices were prominent. In 1971, *Earth's Daughters*, a feminist literary magazine which endures to this day, was established. Jimmie was one of the earliest members of the collective that took over management of the magazine when it became too much for the original three founders to do on their own. She was co-editor of the prestigious journal from 1975–86, devoting much time and energy to bringing other women's voices to the public.

Jimmie was not as forthcoming with her own work. Although a prolific writer, she found it difficult to put her own work out into the world. She frequently wrote about difficult subjects and found it terrifying to be so revealing. She published just three slender volumes during her lifetime: *The Rime and Roar of Revolution* (with Bob Dickens, 1975), *Ain't No Bears Out Tonight* (1984), and *Pieces of Bread* (1987). *Torn from the Ear of Night* has been twenty years in the making, largely due to Jimmie's reluctance to reveal things she feared would distress her family. When she realized, for instance, that her ancestors had been slave owners, she felt a strong compulsion to acknowledge their part in a shameful past and to apologize for it. She wrestled with this, agonized over it, and suffered in the knowledge that it was part of who she was. Ultimately, she believed that although we are all bruised by the cruelty in the world, we need to transcend it and be more than our own suffering. Her exquisite response to this part of her legacy appears in these pages.

But Jimmie has also created another legacy: her work as mentor to so many people, both young and old, who found themselves in one of her classes or workshops. She recognized the importance of Debora Ott's early support, and paid it forward, challenging her students and helping them create meaning for their lives. Anyone who ever spent time with Jimmie realized that she somehow seemed to have as much time as necessary for you. She looked directly at you and spoke in a quiet voice that made you lean in and be still. It was in that stillness that you saw most clearly how to be present in your own life, how to listen to yourself.

Jimmie's work did not go unnoticed. She served as Just Buffalo Writer in Residence for poetry, received The President's Award for Excellence in Teaching at Erie Community College, and won the National Organization for Women's Women Helping Women Award. She was also the founder and first director of the Erie Community College City Campus Women's Center.

In 1980, Jimmie and Geri, both of whom loved ritual and celebrations, had a commitment ceremony at the Delaware Water Gap, a fitting and symbolic location on the northernmost ridge of the Appalachian Mountains. In 2009, they traveled to nearby Niagara-on-the Lake in Ontario, where same sex marriage was legal, and were married. They followed this up with a church blessing in Buffalo. In 2015, same sex marriage was finally legalized in New York, and Jimmie and Geri once again wed—after more than thirty years together.

In September 2015, following a hard-fought battle with cancer, Jimmie was in hospice. A large painting of her beloved Blue Ridge Mountains had been hung on the wall of her room. Geri invited all of Jimmie's friends and students to come gather around her to say goodbye. "When I get stronger, we'll finish that book," or "When I'm feeling better, we'll get started on that project," Jimmie told them. She died on September 24 as she had lived: on her own terms and sharing her great hope, great optimism, and great presence with others.

In an interview done for StoryCorps in September, 2016, a year after Jimmie's death, Laurie Dean Torrell, director of Just Buffalo Literary Center, told Geri that she and Jimmie had been role models for her and asked if she and Jimmie ever had a sense of themselves as pioneers or role models as two women together. "Absolutely not," Geri replied. "We never saw ourselves as *two women* in love. We saw ourselves as two spirits deeply attracted and passionately connected in mind, body, heart, and soul."

—Elaine LaMattina

White Pine Press, Geri Grossman, and the family of Jimmie Margaret Gilliam thank the following individuals for their generous support in the publication of this collection:

Mark and Jocena Avery and Family
Ansie Baird
F. Cindy Baire
Nancy Barnes
Eras Bechakas
Robert Bell
Carole Bellanca
Kathleen Betsko
Maryann Bonner, The Main Attraction
Lawrence and Carolyn Brooks
Arlene Burrows
Gabrielle and Roger Burton and Five Sisters Productions
Rev. Sarah Buxton-Smith
Jen and Mary Callaghan
Debby Cambria
Aidan and Jennifer Chalk
Dan Cook
John DaVanzo
Robert Day and Carolyn Likely
Shelby Deck and Timothy Vukelic
Alexis DeVeaux
Miriam Dow
Linda Drajem
Diane DuBois and Elizabeth Rutherford
Barbara Faust
Sally A Fiedler
Bill Fisher
Christine and Al Franken and Family
Anthony Gattuso, Anthony NY Salon and Staff
Susan Gervase
Marjorie Girth
Gene and Virginia Grabiner
Bea Grossman

Geri Grossman
Michael and Genevieve Grossman and Family
Theresa Stephan Hains
Catherine Herrick
Lorna Hill
Jeff and Shelly Hirshberg
Grey Hodges
Paul and Barbara Hogan
Ruth Kirstein and Art Efron
Jimmy and LeAnn Kiser and Family
Charles and Louise Kreiger
Robert and Mary Kresse
Joe and Cindy Kreuz
Janet Kaye and Dan Kushel
Betsy Kyger
Daniel and Jill (Marea Cheval) Leavitt
Jefferey and Pamela Johnson
Dennis Maloney and Elaine LaMattina
Ann Monroe
Joan and Jim Murray
Virginia and John Oehler
Jimmy and LeAnn Olliff Kiser and Family
Jody and Joe Olliff
Joe and Anna Carson Olliff III and Family
Debora Ott
Karen and Richard Penfold
Daria Pierce
Kristen M. Pope
Rose Roberts and Family
Gary Earl Ross and Tamara Alsace
Lorraine Stern
Trudy Stern and Michael Morgulis
Mary Taglieri
Laurie Dean Torrell and Marvin Henchbarger
Sue Weidermann
Max Wickert
John Wilson
Women of the Crooked Circle